WITHDRAWN

# SEIZURE-ALERT DOGS

## by Margaret Fetty

Consultant: Karen Shirk
Executive Director, 4 Paws For Ability, Inc.

BEARPORT
PUBLISHING

New York, New York

## Credits

Cover and Title Page, © AP Images/The Gleaner/Mike Lawrence; Cover(RT), © Eric Camden; Cover(RM), © Eric Camden; Cover(RB), © Photographers Choice/SuperStock; TOC, © AP Images/ The Gleaner/Mike Lawrence; 4, Courtesy of Jewl Wall; 5, Courtesy of Jewl Wall; 6, © Eric Camden; 7, © Eric Camden; 8, © Bart Rötgens; 9, © AP Images/The Daily Press/Sangjib Min; 10, Courtesy of Canine Partners for Life; 11, © Photographers Choice/SuperStock; 12L, © Eric Camden; 12R, © Eric Camden; 13, © Eric Camden; 14, © Purestock/Lisette Le Bon/SuperStock; 15, © Chris Zuppa/St. Petersburg Times/ZUMA Press; 16, © Paw Prints Pet Photography; 17, © Paw Prints Pet Photography; 18, ©Tom Uhlman/Alamy; 19, Courtesy of 4 Paws For Ability; 20, © Paw Prints Pet Photography; 21, © Paw Prints Pet Photography; 22, Courtesy of Carrie Harpole; 23, Courtesy of Carrie Harpole; 24, Courtesy of Joel Davis & Toad Hall Press. With Alex by my Side © 2000 by Joel Davis. Cover photo by Nancy Collins Davis, © 1999 by Joel Davis & Nancy Collins Davis; 25, Courtesy of Carrie Harpole; 26, © AP Images/The Gleaner/Mike Lawrence; 27, © Paw Prints Pet Photography; 29TL, © thecreativeeyes/ Shutterstock; 29TR, © Pelana/Shutterstock; 29BL, © Eric Isselée/Shutterstock; 29BR, © Eric Isselée/ Shutterstock; 31, © Courtesy of 4 Paws For Ability.

Publisher: Kenn Goin
Senior Editor: Lisa Wiseman
Creative Director: Spencer Brinker
Design: Dawn Beard Creative
Photo Researcher: Amy Dunleavy

*Library of Congress Cataloging-in-Publication Data*

Fetty, Margaret.
  Seizure-alert dogs / by Margaret Fetty ; consultant, Karen Shirk.
    p. cm. — (Dog heroes)
  Includes bibliographical references and index.
  ISBN-13: 978-1-59716-865-6 (library binding)
  ISBN-10: 1-59716-865-3 (library binding)
  1. Animals as aids for people with disabilities—Juvenile literature. 2. Epileptics—Treatment—Juvenile literature. 3. Dogs—Therapeutic use—Juvenile literature. I. Title.
  HV1569.6.F48 2010
  362.196'85308—dc22
                      2009012659

For more information, write to Bearport Publishing Company, Inc., 101 Fifth Avenue, Suite 6R, New York, New York 10003. Printed in the United States of America.

10 9 8 7 6 5 4 3 2 1

# Table of Contents

# Warning in the Park

Jewl Wall and her husband, Michael, were looking for a shady place to rest while enjoying the day at a Georgia theme park. Tagert, Jewl's Labrador retriever, walked alongside them. Suddenly, a crowd swarmed from behind, separating Jewl and Tagert from Michael.

As Jewl looked around for her husband, Tagert nipped her hand. Jewl knew what that meant. A **seizure** was coming! Shortly, she would lose **consciousness** and wouldn't know where she was.

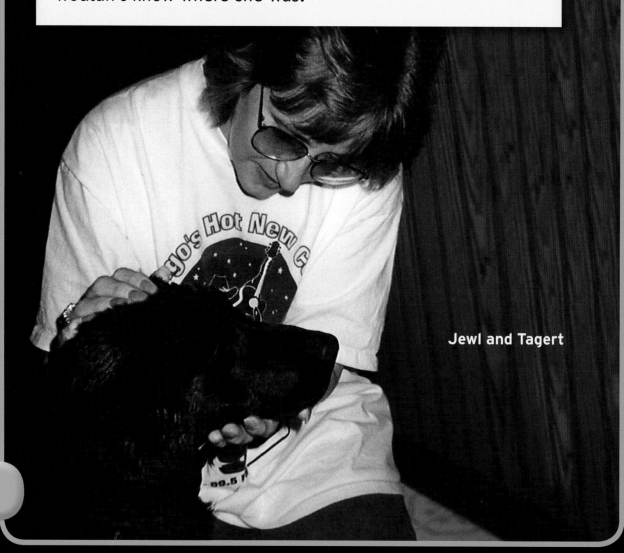

**Jewl and Tagert**

Jewl quickly led her dog behind a game booth where she thought she would be safe. Almost immediately, the seizure struck! Unaware of what she was doing, Jewl started to walk away. Tagert jumped in front of her and stopped her.

For eight minutes, Tagert circled Jewl. No matter which way she turned, the Lab blocked her path. He knew that Jewl had lost consciousness and didn't know what she was doing. When the seizure finally passed, Jewl realized that she was still behind the booth. Tagert had kept her safe!

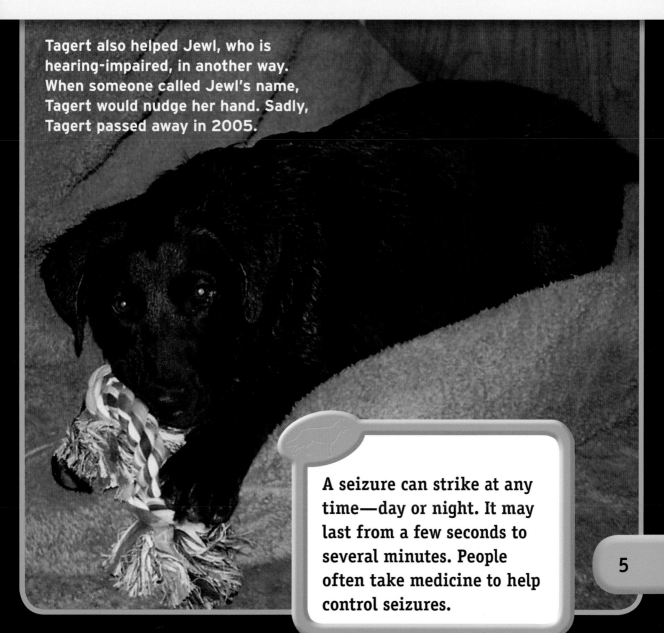

Tagert also helped Jewl, who is hearing-impaired, in another way. When someone called Jewl's name, Tagert would nudge her hand. Sadly, Tagert passed away in 2005.

A seizure can strike at any time—day or night. It may last from a few seconds to several minutes. People often take medicine to help control seizures.

# Brain Signals

Tagert was a seizure-**alert** dog, which means he had been trained to warn people who have **epilepsy** of an oncoming seizure. During a seizure, the brain sends out signals that cause a person to feel and act differently than normal.

Candice, who has epilepsy, gets help crossing the crosswalk from her seizure-alert dog, Chiper.

Seizures can affect people in many ways. Some lose consciousness and fall down, often breaking bones. Parts of their bodies may shake, too. Others, like Jewl, walk around unaware of where they're going. For example, a person might walk into the middle of a busy street. When a seizure-alert dog warns his or her human partner of a seizure, the person has time to prepare and stay safe.

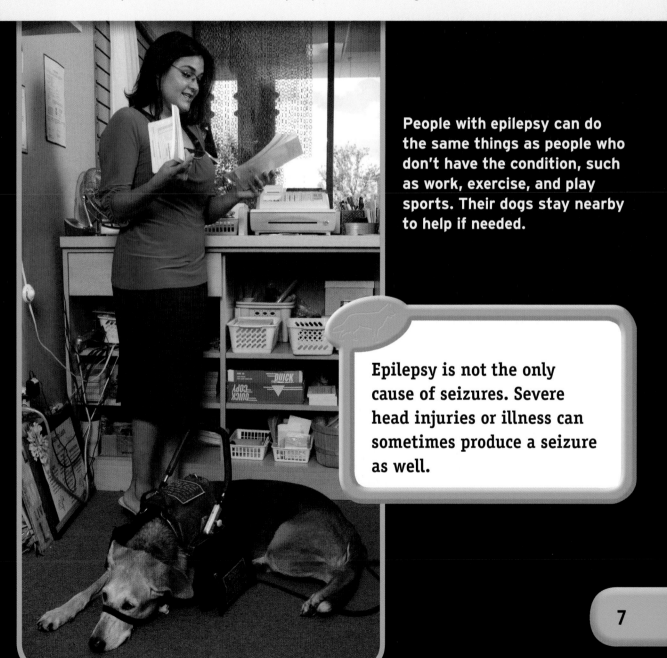

People with epilepsy can do the same things as people who don't have the condition, such as work, exercise, and play sports. Their dogs stay nearby to help if needed.

Epilepsy is not the only cause of seizures. Severe head injuries or illness can sometimes produce a seizure as well.

# A Helping Paw

Many seizure-alert dogs such as Tagert are also seizure-response dogs. These **canines** perform tasks that help their partners during seizures. For example, after Tagert nipped Jewl's hand to tell her that a seizure was coming, he responded to the situation by circling Jewl so she wouldn't walk away.

This seizure-response dog demonstrates how he lies on top of his human partner so that he will not get up and walk away during a seizure.

Seizure-response dogs are trained to help protect their partners in many other ways. Some know to move objects out of their partner's path to prevent the person from falling or bumping into something dangerous. Others learn to use their heads or paws to flip a special switch in their home that's connected to a 911 emergency service. That way the dog can get help whenever his or her partner is in trouble.

A dog demonstrates hitting a special button to contact emergency help.

**Service dogs** are trained to help people. Seizure-alert and seizure-response dogs, as well as guide dogs, hearing dogs, and **mobility dogs**, are kinds of service dogs.

# Knowing to Alert

No one is sure how seizure-alert dogs know that a seizure will strike. Most dog trainers believe that changes in a person's body before and during a seizure make a slight odor that dogs can smell. After all, a canine's ability to smell is 1,000 times better than a human's!

A service dog can be any breed of dog, male or female, and any age.

Seizure-alert dogs often warn their partners anywhere from 15 to 45 minutes before the seizure starts. Some dogs can warn up to twelve hours in advance.

Trainers also believe that dogs strongly **bonded** to their human partners are likely to be the best alert dogs. These animals notice any change, however small, in their partners' behavior. For instance, a person's eyes may flutter just before a seizure starts. Over time, the dog learns that this flutter means a seizure is about to begin.

Dogs and their owners often have very close relationships.

# Paws with Personality

A dog that helps people with seizures needs a good personality. He or she must be friendly, easily getting along with other animals and people. These dogs also need to enjoy visiting new places, and they need to be smart because they will have to master many skills.

SEIZURE ALERT DOG
If My Owner Has a Seizure
1. Do Not Separate Us
2. Do Not Call an Ambulance Unless the Seizure Lasts More Than 5 Minutes Or Injury Has Occurred

This patch tells people that a dog is a seizure-alert dog.

Do Not Pet or Distract Working Service Dog

Seizure-alert dogs, like all service dogs, should wear a cape with a patch that shows they are trained to help people.

For example, the dog will have to learn to **focus**. Food, smells, noises, and other people must not **distract** the animal from noticing the signs of an oncoming seizure in his or her partner. The dog also needs to learn to be well behaved at all times, especially during emergencies.

People should ask before petting a service dog. It's important that the dog stays focused on his or her human partner.

# A Good Beginning

A seizure-alert dog is only a few days old when training begins. **Volunteers** hold and play with the puppy so it will get used to being around people.

At about two months of age, the pup goes to live with a puppy raiser. This person teaches the dog simple **commands**, such as "sit" and "stay."

Holding and playing with puppies helps them get used to being with people.

To get used to different sounds, big crowds, and many kinds of smells, the pup goes everywhere with the puppy raiser. The little animal may visit offices, stores, and parks, or ride on trains and buses with the puppy raiser. All these experiences prepare the dog for a life of service.

Many prisons have programs in which inmates train puppies that will become service dogs.

Inmates at a prison in Florida work with dogs in an eight-week training program.

# Seizure Training

At about one year of age, the dog leaves the puppy raiser and goes to a training center, such as 4 Paws For Ability in Xenia, Ohio. There, a trainer helps the pup learn to identify the **scent** that signals the start of a seizure. Then the trainer teaches the dog how to warn the human that the scent has been detected.

Trainers such as Jennifer (left) often have the dogs train with people who have epilepsy.

Jennifer, who trains dogs at 4 Paws, knows that when an animal sniffs excitedly at someone just before a seizure begins, it has learned to recognize the scent. Jennifer watches to see how the animal chooses to alert—some paw, others bark. She rewards the dog with food and praise after each alert. This helps the dog learn to repeat the action.

Though Tagert alerted Jewl by gently nipping her hand, most dogs today are taught to alert by pawing or barking. Here Jeremy, another trainer at 4 Paws, works with a seizure-alert dog on how to alert by pawing.

It may cost up to $20,000 to train one seizure-alert dog.

# A Perfect Match

While the dogs are learning important skills, their trainers begin to match them with human partners. If a person likes outdoor activities such as hiking, for example, a dog with lots of energy is the best match. A quiet dog is a better partner for a person who enjoys staying at home most of the time. To help with the match, people who want a seizure-alert dog first must answer questions about their **lifestyle**.

Dogs with lots of energy can make great companions while hiking.

Once a match is made, the human partner sends some of his or her old clothes to the trainers. These items have a scent that is **unique** to the person. The dog is allowed to sleep with the clothes to learn the person's smell, which is the first step in building a bond between the dog and future owner.

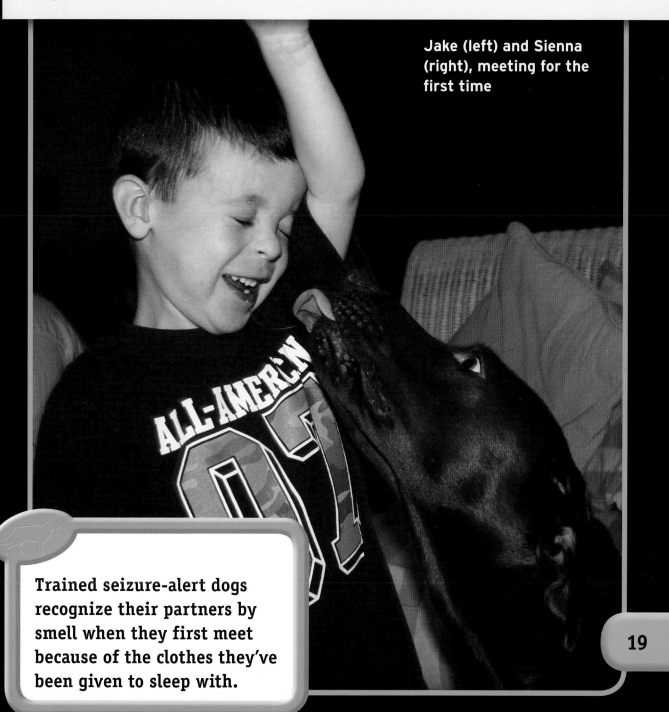

Jake (left) and Sienna (right), meeting for the first time

Trained seizure-alert dogs recognize their partners by smell when they first meet because of the clothes they've been given to sleep with.

# Team Training

Once people are matched with a seizure-alert dog from 4 Paws For Ability, they go to a team-training camp. There, they meet their new canine partners. For the next ten days, the human partners learn commands so that they can **communicate** with their dogs. One of the first commands is "down-stay." These words tell the dogs to lie down and stay very still.

Human partners and their dogs in a training session at 4 Paws

During team training, the dogs learn, too. If a human partner has a seizure at camp, trainers guide the dog to use the skills that he or she has learned to help the person. Food rewards are given each time the dog alerts after recognizing the person's unique pre-seizure behavior. Before long, the human and dog are a team!

Seizure-alert dogs, like all service dogs, can legally go anywhere that people go, including restaurants, movie theaters, and malls.

Jeremy takes a seizure-alert dog team to the mall so that the dog and the human learn how to work together in a public place.

# Team Alex and Lady

With the help of 4 Paws For Ability, Alex Harpole, who has epilepsy, was paired with Lady, a German shepherd. Since completing camp, Alex and Lady go everywhere together. When Alex plays basketball or goes to school, Lady is right beside him. Lady even sleeps in Alex's bed at night to make sure he stays safe.

Lady knows when Alex (right) will have a seizure about 40 minutes before it starts. When she senses one, she finds an adult and paws to alert.

The two friends have even traveled to Washington, D.C., so Alex could share his story with members of the U.S. Congress. There, Alex and others worked to get Congress to pass laws to help people with epilepsy. One law gives extra money to programs that encourage the early detection and treatment of epilepsy for people who don't have access to doctors.

Lady, Alex (in the light blue sweater), and his family met with Congressman Ed Whitfield (far left) from Kentucky during their trip to Washington, D.C.

In October 2008, seven people climbed Mt. Everest, the tallest mountain in the world, in honor of Alex and Lady. They wanted to draw attention to epilepsy and teach people about the condition.

# A Small Wonder

Not all seizure-alert dogs learn their skills from a trainer. Alex, a miniature Dachshund, belongs to Joel Davis and his family. This small dog is quick to warn Joel when he senses that a seizure is coming. Yet Alex hasn't had any scent training. So how does Alex alert?

with **ALEX** by my side

"Joel Davis has written a story that is personal and passionate, and beautifully describes the special relationship he shares with Alex, his seizure-alert dog. Joel chronicles the challenges he faces as an epileptic, his constant efforts to educate the public about what a service dog does, and how his life-changing disability defines his work and his world. More than a 'pet,' Alex is an unexpected blessing in the Davis family's life, and *With Alex by My Side* is the tale of love, devotion and courage of a Miniature Dachshund and the human he helps."

—Vicki Kung, Co-Founder, Dogpark.com

**Joel Davis**

This is the cover of the book Joel Davis wrote about his experiences with Alex.

Joel noticed that Alex would jump up and wildly lick his face before a seizure. Or if they were in different rooms, Alex would suddenly run into Joel's room and wrap his paws around his master's legs. Joel soon realized that Alex was warning him that a seizure was coming. Nowadays, when Alex alerts, Joel immediately takes medicine to block the coming seizure.

**Seizure-alert dogs are taught to stay close to their human partners during and after a seizure. This helps a person feel safe and calm during a seizure.**

# Canine Heroes

Like Joel Davis, Alex Harpole now knows when a seizure will strike. Before Lady came along, he wasn't able to do a lot of things that his friends were doing because he might have a seizure and fall. Now Alex and Lady go many places together. Alex knows that he will be safe because Lady will warn him.

Alex and Lady

Lady has changed Alex's life. Like all seizure-alert dogs, Lady is a true hero. She always puts Alex's safety first, while also offering him friendship, love, and **confidence**. Such wonderful gifts help people with epilepsy live **independent** lives.

Stika, a graduate of 4 Paws For Ability, is just one of many special dogs that helps people with epilepsy live their lives to the fullest.

Some researchers believe that a dog's friendship with a person who has epilepsy can be so reassuring and calming that it may cut down on the number of seizures that the person has.

# Just the Facts

- Many dogs chosen for seizure-alert and seizure-response work are found in animal shelters. Before they are chosen, they are carefully checked for good health and calmness.

- Service dogs work all the time. Like overworked people, they may feel stress. To help them stay in good mental and physical health, they need plenty of playtime and exercise.

- Karen Shirk started 4 Paws For Ability. She needed a service dog to help her when the muscles in her body became very weak. No training center would give her a dog, though. So she trained a German shepherd named Ben to help her. Karen believes that anyone who wants a service dog should have one, no matter what kind of disease or condition a person has.

- On September 7, 2004, Leana Beasley took some medicine that made her very sick. Faith, her seizure-alert dog, pushed the phone off the base and hit a button that was programmed to dial 911. She barked into the phone to get help. Then she used her response skills to roll Leana into a safe position. When the police arrived, Faith unlocked the door and led the police to Leana. Faith received the **American Kennel Club** Service Dog Award in 2005 for saving Leana's life.

# Common Breeds: Seizure-Alert Dogs

Labrador retriever

German shepherd

mixed breed

golden retriever

**alert** (uh-LURT) ready to warn someone of danger such as an oncoming seizure; on guard

**American Kennel Club** (uh-MER-i-kuhn KEN-uhl KLUHB) a national organization that is involved in many activities having to do with dogs, including collecting information about dog breeds and setting rules for dog shows

**bonded** (BOND-id) connected with someone; a close friendship

**canines** (KAY-nyenz) members of the dog family

**commands** (kuh-MANDZ) instructions given to be obeyed; orders

**communicate** (kuh-MYOO-nuh-kate) to share information, wants, needs, and feelings

**confidence** (KON-fuh-duhnss) when a person has a strong belief in his or her own ability

**consciousness** (KON-shuhss-ness) the state of being awake, alert, and able to think

**distract** (diss-TRAKT) to keep from paying attention to something

**epilepsy** (EP-uh-*lep*-see) a medical condition of the brain that causes seizures

**focus** (FOH-kuhss) to keep one's concentration on something

**independent** (in-di-PEN-duhnt) able to do things without help

**lifestyle** (LIFE-*stile*) a way of living that reflects a person's values and attitudes

**mobility dogs** (moh-BIL-i-tee DAWGZ) dogs that help people who use wheelchairs or need aid walking

**scent** (SENT) a smell or odor

**seizure** (SEE-zhur) a sudden attack that can cause a person to shake and even lose consciousness

**service dogs** (SUR-viss DAWGZ) dogs that are trained to help people do daily tasks

**unique** (yoo-NEEK) one of a kind; like no other

**volunteers** (*vol*-uhn-TIHRZ) people who offer to do a job without getting paid

## Bibliography

**Bunnell, Melissa, and Marci Davis.** *Working Like Dogs: The Service Guide Book.* Crawford, CO: Alpine Publications (2007).

**Davis, Joel.** *With Alex by My Side.* Laceyville, PA: Toad Hall Press (2000).

## Read More

**Mink, Lisa.** *Koko the Service Dog.* Bloomington, IN: Author House (2008).

**Ruffin, Frances E.** *Medical Detective Dogs (Dog Heroes).* New York: Bearport Publishing (2007).

**Singer, Marilyn.** *A Dog's Gotta Do What a Dog's Gotta Do: Dogs at Work.* New York: Henry Holt (2000).

## Learn More Online

Visit these Web sites to learn more about seizure-alert dogs:

**www.4pawsforability.org**

**www.canineassistants.org**

**www.epilepsyfoundation.org/kidsclub/nonflash/home/index.html**

## Index

## About the Author

Margaret Fetty lives in Austin, Texas, with her two miniature schnauzers, Cabo and Tristian. All three enjoy long runs in the park.

## DATE DUE

| | |
|---|---|
| AUG 1 9 2011 | |
| | |
| JAN – 8 2014 | |
| Jan. 29, 2014 | |
| | |
| OCT 1 7 2014 | |
| FEB 2 1 2017 | |
| | |
| | |
| | |
| | |
| | |

DEMCO, INC. 38-2931